Published by Patrician Press 2016
For more information: www.patricianpress.com

Martin Johnson has worked in education throughout his career, completing his main career with the Further Education Unit, a government-supported think-tank where he had responsibility at different times for publications and research. He read English at Emmanuel College, Cambridge and has previously published only work on education.

Robert Macfarlane's
Orphans

Robert Macfarlane's Orphans

Poems borrowed
by
Martin Johnson

Patrician Press • Manningtree

First published as a paperback edition by Patrician
Press 2016

British Library Cataloguing in Publication Data. A
catalogue record for this book is available from the
British Library.

ISBN 978-0-9932388-7-1

Printed and bound in Peterborough by
Printondemand-worldwide

www.patricianpress.com

Introduction

This small book is a collection of poems most of which take as their inspiration the recent best-selling and brilliant book, *The Old Ways* by Robert Macfarlane. Most of the words in the poems are drawn directly from his text, though re-arranged. The poems stem directly from a challenge to Macfarlane at a recent public lecture that he, like Edward Thomas, his great favourite, should release the poetry that lay undiscovered in his prose. The challenge was declined, so this author (the challenger) decided to take it up himself.

As well as *The Old Ways*, a direct contributor to the impetus leading to this quest was another well-received book about Edward Thomas, *Now All Roads Lead to France* by Matthew Hollis. In this book, the author describes what led to Thomas's poems, all written in the last years of his life, before he was killed by the blast of a shell in 1917. The alchemical process that led to Thomas's late flowering as a poet was catalysed by his friendship with Robert Frost who encouraged Thomas to believe he was already a poet and had simply to release his poems from their prosaic fetters.

Despite his Welsh origins, there is a sort of untainted Englishness about Edward Thomas. As a poet of the countryside and the natural world, he has few equals. Many readers stop at that definition of his poetry and miss much. Robert Macfarlane tells us how, when he first read him as a young man, he seemed 'an engagingly simple author, verging on the naïve: an elegist for a rural

England of ploughmen, hayricks and meadowsweet, that was vanishing even as he wrote.'[1]

What he recognised years later was that Thomas's central concerns were 'disconnection, discrepancy and unsettledness'[2]. There are similar features in some of Macfarlane's writing: who is it but the 'unsettled' that endlessly follow 'old ways'?

Thomas's career as a poet was remarkable, the whole body of his output confined to a handful of years, and yet he is regarded today as one of the most influential of twentieth century poets, Ted Hughes's phrase 'the father of us all', the best-known accolade.

And yet much of his early work was conceived in anguish: he was a depressive who punished all around him, particularly his wife Helen, for the labour of his work. His early years as a writer were spent on reviewing others' work and writing about the countryside, work which, though admired by many, barely paid the rent.

Matthew Hollis shows in detail how Thomas's poem 'Up in the Wind' emerged from notes in an exercise book intended as a draft for a prose piece[3]. His most famous poem 'Adlestrop', which especially qualifies for Ivor Gurney's description of Thomas's poems as 'nebulously, intangibly beautiful', similarly emerged from prose notes.

The notion that poems can be unlocked from prose passages is not much explored. Classic definitions of poetry like Wordsworth's 'emotion recollected in tranquillity', Yeats's notions of inspiration or Dylan

1   Robert Macfarlane 'The Old Ways' pp24-5
2   Ibid p25
3   Matthew Hollis 'Now All Roads Lead To France' pp184ff

Thomas's painstaking revisions of what appears spontaneous do not allow this sort of conception of poetry writing. Indeed prose and poetry are usually regarded as quite distinct as genres, with no examples of poems which have earlier prose drafts.

Asking for 'meaning' or a prose equivalent from a poem is usually regarded as a literary solecism, so why should a reverse process be admissible?

It could, however, be postulated that the kind of prose from which poems might emerge, would be imaginative and figurative: less functional, more allusive, the language of Ecclesiastes: 'To everything there is a season', or *The Messiah*: 'The Lord God omnipotent reigneth'. At the recent public lecture mentioned above in which Professor John Mullan introduced a discussion about *The Old Ways*, when the author, Macfarlane, was challenged to work the same trick with his own very poetical prose he modestly dismissed the challenge as beyond his powers, his early efforts at writing poetry having been, for him, unsatisfactory.

This short book is an attempt to demonstrate that writing poetry in this way is legitimate, and that it can be possible even for a third party to use another's prose writing as a mine for poems of his or her own. It is not an academic work but something that arises from a lifelong love of Edward Thomas's poems, recently stimulated by a couple of wonderful books as well as a fascination with the structures of poetry and what inspires its creation. It also relates the poems to their originating prose passages with comments on the creation of the poems.

So who wrote these poems? Clearly Edward Thomas owned both the prose notes from which his poems derived and the poems themselves. Most of the following poems rely both on the words from another's writing, and the inspiration that gave rise to the poems, which undoubtedly arose for this writer from the skills of Robert Macfarlane. And yet those words have been re-arranged, edited, altered or reversed. Meaning has inevitably been changed in some cases to an extent that the original author would not acknowledge the poem's intention to be his at all. One of the poems derives from Edward Thomas's words in *The Icknield Way* and another in part from a quotation used by Macfarlane from Rebecca West, but most use Macfarlane's own words as inspiration. The first part of the collection ends with a poem which, though my own, was stimulated by a chapter in *The Old Ways*, and borrows a few words from Macfarlane, 'the mirrored world', 'nothing is itself'.

The last three poems are drawn from *Landmarks* (2015). Two are entirely dependent on words in the text (which were not, originally, Macfarlane's own), and the other takes as its inspiration the story of the deletions from the new edition of the *Oxford Junior Dictionary*.

All of this led to a quandary about permission and copyright. What would Robert Macfarlane say? Are words that are re-arranged still owned by their author? I wonder if Wendy Cope got permission for her title *Making Cocoa for Kingsley Amis*, an eye-catching title that no doubt sold a few copies on its own. How would a title like *Robert Macfarlane's Orphans* go down with the author of *The Old Ways*? Perhaps I should dedicate the book to his three proper children by way of apology. Would he think I was simply jumping on the speeding bandwagon that his writing career has become and maybe increasing my own sales as a result? What chutzpah from a novice writer, known only to a few for educational writing!

As the midwife to these poems, I would recommend they should be read before the prose extracts from which they derive. I hope that the poems are also worth reading as 'original' work and not just as part of a literary experiment. I considered relegating the extracts and the commentary to appendices to make the poems more likely to be read for themselves. However, I decided this would suggest that the primary purpose of the book is to offer a collection of new poetry, when my true purpose is to explore a new seam, to make the reader think about how poetry gets written. Few poets publish collections of poetry with explanatory notes (*The Waste Land* a rare exception), and it is a risk to do this, most writers of poetry preferring not to demystify for good reasons. So, I take this risk and offer the book as a genuine tribute to *The Old Ways* and Robert Macfarlane and in honour of someone we both love, Edward Thomas.

So I, an unknown hack possibly as close to my end as Edward Thomas was when he began to write his poems, threw myself on Robert Macfarlane's mercy and asked for permission to use his work in this way. This was (part of) his reply:

'I am warmly grateful for the attention you've paid to my prose, and the fossil poems you've prised from the strata of my paragraphs. And perhaps above all by the alignments you've found between my writing/sensibility, and that of the man and poet we both admire so much, Edward Thomas. I read your 'Orphans' with pleasure and a smile, enjoying the generous care of the introduction, and then the ingenuities of the poem-pages that followed, with their creative elisions, omissions and reconfigurings. Certainly, you sprang newness from what are, to me, some very familiar lines!'

A gracious and generous response. So the book is dedicated to Robert's children, and to mine.

The Old Ways (TOW) p273

'So it was down, steeply down, across shale slopes, the stones of the path flowing in the sunlight, the horses skidding on their front hooves, braking with their back hooves, deerskin bags lurching forward on their flanks, their bells tolling rapid alarm. We came on behind, tracing a stream-cut as it plunged off the pass, following it between saplings of pine and Himalayan oak and through bushes of rhododendron, stumbling in powdered snow that reached knee-deep in places. The stream was part frozen, halted mid-leap in elaborate forms of yearning- chandeliers, ink-flicks and hat feathers. On the west side of the valley, the tops of distant oaks shone like brass in the sunlight. A small bright bird flew to a gnarled pine. I sat with my back against the warm wall, facing the sun and the mountain, narrowing my eyes.'

Not much to say here except that the poem appeared to be calling to me. Read the prose passage: the poem is there, isn't it? Rearrangement does make minor changes to the meaning: for example 'narrowing my eyes' reaches back to the sun. Is it the cause or the consequence, an ambiguity that may tease?

Miles to go

So it was down, steeply down,
across shale slopes,
stones flowing in the sunlight,
horses skidding on front hooves,
braking with back hooves,
deerskin bags lurching forward
bells tolling rapid alarm.
Tracing a stream-cut
as it plunged off the pass,
through saplings of pine
and Himalayan oak,
through rhododendron,
stumbling in powdered snow
knee-deep.

Stream part frozen, halted
mid-leap in yearning:
chandeliers, ink-flicks, hat feathers.

To the west
distant oaks shone
brass in the sunlight.

A small bright bird flew to a gnarled pine.

I rested,
my back to the warm wall,
facing the sun
narrowing my eyes.

The Icknield Way - Edward Thomas p144

'He was one of those creatures provided by a mighty providence for attending on that "noble animal" the horse; but this did not prevent him from calling his own horse John "old son". He never carried a whip, because, he said, he did not believe in hurting "dumb animals". A man who knows horses well is equally at home in town or country, and although this man was as full-blooded a Cockney as his wife, he was, like her, contented with his three or four years of country solitude; it was, he said, "a happy life, yes, a happy life"...

'I asked him about *The Icknield Way*... he had heard a man could walk on it for twelve months and come back to the same place again...

'I fell asleep...while the stone curlews were piping on the downs and a pair of country wheels were rolling by, late and slow.'

This poem is drawn from Thomas's best-known prose work. It does feel a little Thomas-like, if that is not too hubristic, with the dying fall at the end of the poem. Think of Thomas's waking up poem, Cock Crow's last line: 'The milkers lace their boots up at the farms.'

The Landlord

Was given by a mighty providence
To tend his horse 'old son'.

'Old son' was never whipped. My host,
A little active man, a Cockney countryman
Knew the Icknield Way, he'd heard
A man could walk it and come back
To where he started
A twelvemonth later and he had
A happy life, a happy life.

I fell asleep.
Stone curlews piping on the downs.

A pair of country wheels rolled by, late and slow.

TOW p340

'Paths and tracks criss-cross his own work, figuratively and structurally. He writes of winding roads and he writes in winding syntax…
'Again and again, in Thomas's imagination, text and landscape overlap: "The prettiest things on ground are the paths/With morning and evening hobnails dinted,/ With foot and wingtip overprinted/Or separately charactered." The paths are sentences, the shod feet of travellers the scratch of the pen-nib or the press of the type.'

Here two of Thomas's own lines quoted by Macfarlane interpose his own words and the poem, by concentrating the point being made by Robert suggests a kind of comparison between Thomas's poetic prose and his own.

Paths and tracks

Paths and tracks criss-cross his work
Winding roads and winding syntax:
'With foot and wing-tip overprinted
Or separately charactered'.

The paths are sentences, the shod feet
The scratch of nib or press of type.

TOW p336

'The work is hard, a bill-paying hackery, that leaves him exhausted and despondent. His changes of mood are weather-like, and at times provoked by the weather… When the black days arrive he lashes out at Helen… "I hate my work," he writes in a letter… Helen waits patiently "to be let into the light again" and meets his cruelty with an unquerying acceptance of his right to be cruel.'

This simply concentrates 69 words into 29, focussing attention on Thomas's tyrannical moods and Helen's supine but heroic compliance.

Helen

His labour's hard
His moods the weather
Some days are black
He hates his work,
Lashes her,
Cruelty his right.

She waits in patience,
To feel his light again.

TOW p337

'When he's happy? Oh, then the days are fine. The house is filled with stories and rhymes… His voice is deep and his songs are various.'

Just a few phrases picked from a slightly longer passage picturing the other side of Edward.

His moods

When he's happy
Oh, then the days are fine
The house filled with rhyme
And stories; his voice deep,
His songs various.

TOW p318

'I heard the first scream at around two o'clock in the morning. A high-pitched and human cry, protracted but falling away in its closing phase. It came from the opposite side of the tree ring to where I was sleeping. My thoughts were sleep-muddled: A child in distress? A rabbit being taken by a weasel or a fox? Impossible though: the sound was coming from at least tree-top height. A bird, then; an owl, surely... Then another cry joined the first, different in tone and more grainy; rising at its end; the shriek of a blade laid hard to a lathe.

'Then I realised that the voices had split and were now coming towards me: still at treetop height but circling round the tree ring, one clockwise and one anticlockwise... After fifteen minutes they stopped and eventually, uneasily, I fell back to sleep...

'Most worryingly close to my own experience was a testimony from 1966, when a group of bikers had spent the night at the Ring. Things were quiet until after midnight, when a crackling sound started, followed by the wailing voice of a woman that appeared to move around the circumference of the Ring. The motorcyclists fled...'

This, along with the description of the Broomway walk, is one of the most evocative stories in The Old Ways. On this occasion, there is little doubt that the short poem is not an adequate substitute for the original text (nor was it intended to be). It can't tell the tale with the same degree of dread. In fact, it may fail if it cannot be understood without reference to the original text. But poems rarely tell stories, they rather distil experience and offer a sample of something to examine and toy with. It stays in for the reader to toy with.

The Chanctonbury Ring

Sleeping out at night
The first scream at two,
A high-pitched and human cry:
A child?
Surely a dying rabbit?
My thoughts sleep-muddled,
But now treetop height
An owl?
But no! A shriek
Blade on lathe.
A wailing voice
Circling, circling.

An uneasy sleep.

Others had fled.

'On the day of his death the Duke was in a reception hall in his palace in Sarajevo – even as Princip and the other assassins were taking up their positions along the line of the cavalcade – and the walls of the reception hall, wrote [Rebecca] West were: "stuffed all the way up to the crimson and gold vaults and stalactites with the furred and feathered ghosts, set close, because there were so many of them: stags with the air between their antlers stuffed with woodcock, quail, pheasant, partridge, capercailzie, and the like; boars standing bristling flank to flank, the breadth under their broad bellies, packed with layer upon layer of hares and rabbits.

"Their animal eyes, clear and dark as water, would brightly watch the approach of their slayer to an end that exactly resembled their own." '

Material here has been edited and shaped, with the lurking assassin not introduced until after the description of the banquet, to heighten the drama. Editing also has involved here some losses: I found it hard to leave out 'the crimson and gold vaults', and 'stalactites' though striking, didn't fit for me. I also chose to omit 'clear' as a descriptor of water as I fancied the counter-intuitive dark on its own. Also, of course, the poem is drawn from two writers raising a different question about authorship, ownership and whether these are 'original' works or not.

The Archduke's reception

The walls were stuffed with furred and feathered ghosts
Stags with antlers hung with game
Boars bristling flank to flank,
Layers of hares and rabbits.
Their eyes, dark as water,
Watching.

Princip by the cavalcade
Watching.

TOW p179

'The sky was black, trimmed with grey: rain on the way. A lapwing turned and tumbled overhead, making for the coast, letting out wireless bleeps and twiddles.
' "Lapwings have got those lovely spoon-shaped wings," I said. "They're one of my favourite birds."
"Not much flesh on them," said Steve.'

Few changes: just a couple of elisions of words unnecessary for the meaning: 'have got', 'They're one of...'

Lapwings

Sky black, trimmed with grey:
rain on the way.
A lapwing turned and tumbled overhead
Making for the coast
With wireless bleeps and twiddles.
'lovely spoon-shaped wings'
I said. 'A favourite bird'.

'Not much flesh on them'
said Steve.

TOW p346

'Thomas gives Helen a book into which he has copied out all his poems. "Remember that, whatever happens, all is well between us for ever and ever," he tells her. A freezing mist hangs in the air.

'Thomas walks away, the hard snow unmarked by his leaving feet. Helen stands at the gate and watches him go until the mist hides him. As he descends the hill, he keeps on calling coo-ee! to her as if he were arriving rather than leaving. She answers him with her coo-ee! And they go on like that, call and answer, fainter and fainter.'

This one is where it all started for me. 'Fainter and fainter' sounded to me like a deliberate echo of Edward's most loved poem Adlestrop: 'Mistier/Farther and farther, all the birds /Of Oxfordshire and Gloucestershire', a connection not denied by Macfarlane. There are other such echoes in The Old Ways. I nearly added as a last line 'All the Oxfordshires and Gloucestershires', that is, the soldiers of those regiments who died in the same war. But that was maybe a melodramatic step too far, and, in any case, they weren't Edward's regiments. And the diminishing font size? Not sure!

The Last Goodbye

He walks away, the hard snow unmarked.
'All is well between us, for ever and ever.'

She watches till he's hidden by the mist.

Coo-ee he calls,
(As if arriving)

She calls Coo-ee,
(As if greeting)

Again

Again

Fainter and fainter

Mistier

Farther and farther.

The Broomway is a footpath leading from Wakering Stairs in South Essex across tidal mudflats to Foulness Island. Its danger and mystery is hauntingly described in TOW Chapter 4. Further north in Essex is Wrabness, on the beautiful Stour Estuary, where my father, a North Essex vicar, used to take us on muddy walks as children.

Here's one of my own (but inspired by *TOW*).

The Broomway

My father was a cautious man
Who settled early for contentment
After wartime naval service.
On holidays, though, he'd take us kids
A mile or two in sinking mud,
The tide approaching.
Further south the mirrored world:
The Broomway, path of doom,
Nothing is itself, risk the point.
Return a maybe.

A cautious man, myself
Now, old as my late dad,
I yearn for risk, and long for
That sucking, sinking mud.

I think I'll walk the Broomway
And see what I can find.

Finally, three poems drawn from *Landmarks* (Macfarlane 2015)

Landmarks p3

In the first chapter of Landmarks, Macfarlane notes with regret the substitutions made in the new edition of the Oxford Junior Dictionary: 'the outdoor and natural being displaced by the indoor and virtual'. My poem describes and embellishes this regret.

'Ghast', by the way, while conveniently rhyming with past, is here an archaic substantive adjective meaning ghost-like but is also a sinister creature from Minecraft, the sensationally popular video game. Ghasts in Minecraft are 'huge, floating nether mobs that shoot explosive fireballs at the game player'. In an earlier draft I used 'Apple glow', the pallor seen on a young person's face when photographed while using a mobile phone.

'Living fossils' refers to Ralph Waldo Emerson's notion that 'Language is fossil poetry' quoted by Macfarlane on p6 of Landmarks. Emerson sought to restore 'the poetic origin of words'.

The Oxford Junior Dictionary – New Edition

(The OUP explains its deletions)

For blackberry read BlackBerry
For bluebell read blog
For catkin read chatroom.

Goodbye to the conker and cowslip
Farewell to the heron and lark
The newt and the otter and willow
All gone into the dark.

These words are no longer wanted
Children don't need them because
The seasons have lost their authority
You can't feel the weather indoors.

The starlit words that sparkled
Are lost in Apple ghast
Those words are living fossils
We lose them and cancel the past.

Landmarks p30

All the words are originally from 'Moorland Diary' by Anne Campbell, first published in 2007 in 'A-mach an Gleann, A Known Wilderness' (Anne Campbell and Jon Macleod), an artists' book which accompanied an exhibition of the same name (An Lanntair 2007, Taigh Chearsabhagh 2008).

Macfarlane I guess chose to quote these words for their poetic quality. Isolating them from their prose context may enhance this quality.

A Walk in a Known Wilderness

In a long wind carrying birdcalls
Through drifts of sparkling bog-cotton
And scarlet damselflies
We disturbed a hind in long grass
Near greenshank territory.

And stopped at a shieling
Where an eagle had preened.

Landmarks p106

A transcription and re-ordering of the varieties of apples recorded by Roger Deakin in the Girton College orchards. Macfarlane himself describes the list as 'a poem of pomes'.

Apple Varieties in Girton College Garden

Scarlet Pimpernel,
Northern Greening,
Peasgood's Nonsuch,
Norfolk Beefing.

Patricia,
Dr Harvey,
American Mother;

Laxton's Exquisite and
King of the Pippins.

Bibliography

Robert Macfarlane, *The Old Ways* (Hamish Hamilton 2012)

Robert Macfarlane, *Landmarks* (Hamish Hamilton 2015)

Robert Macfarlane, *Original Copy – Plagiarism and Originality in Nineteenth Century Literature* (Oxford University Press 2007)

Matthew Hollis, *Now All Roads Lead to France: The Last Years of Edward Thomas* (Faber and Faber 2011)

Edward Thomas, *The Icknield Way* (Constable 1913)

Acknowledgements/Permissions

An earlier work by Robert Macfarlane was called
Original Copy (OUP 2007) and dealt with plagiarism
and originality in nineteenth century literature. Chapter
2 is called Legitimizing Appropriation. I am grateful
that Robert's permission has legitimized my
appropriation.

Thanks to Rosemary Vellender for her permission to
use the extract from *The Icknield Way*, her grandfather
Edward Thomas's book.

Thanks to the estate of Rebecca West for permission to
use the quotation on which much of 'The Archduke's
Reception' is based.

Thanks to Anne Campbell for permission to use her
words from *A Moorland Diary*.

I am grateful to David and Lorna Unwin and to Esmé
Sillito for reading the draft and offering helpful
suggestions.

I am also grateful to my publisher, Patricia Borlenghi,
for encouraging me and for her valuable advice.

Finally, love and thanks to my wife, Gail, for helping
me to make space for all this in our busy lives!

Other Patrician Press titles include:

Disarming the Porcupine by Mark Brayley
Poetry
Paperback 978-0-9927235-1-4 £7.50 and e-book edition

Four Quartets – T S Eliot and Spirituality by
Richard Brock
Paperback 978-0-99323-880-2 £7.95

Arcobaleno Rainbow by Sara Elena Rossetti
Poetry
Paperback 978-0-9927235-5-2 £7.95 and e-book edition

Three Wishes by Philip Terry
Experimental
Paperback 978-0-9927235-7-6 £5.00 and e-book edition